best of **ani difranco**

PiANo VoCAL GuiTAr

ISBN 0-634-01220-7

7777 W. BLUEMOUND RD. P.O. BOX 13819 MILWAUKEE, WI 53213

Visit Hal Leonard Online at
www.halleonard.com

The 21 songs contained in this volume represent Ani DiFranco's personal selection of highlights of her work from 1990 to early 1999. Unlike earlier Ani songbooks published by Hal Leonard, this one supplies notation for piano as well as guitar, so what you'll find here are the most "piano-friendly" of her compositions. The majority of these songs have never appeared in print before—although a number of tracks from *Little Plastic Castle* and *Up Up Up Up Up Up* can be found here in different form than they did in the songbooks for those albums, which strove to accurately transcribe the recorded versions of the songs. (A companion songbook, *Best of: Guitar,* collects for the first time 20 more of Ani's selections from her initial seven albums transcribed for solo guitar.)

While Ani's approach to songwriting is deeply rooted in the two decades she has spent wielding an acoustic guitar—keyboards did not begin to play a significant role in her work until Julie Wolf joined the touring band in 1998— the current volume demonstrates that many of her earlier compositions are equally at home on the piano. Moreover, Ani's catalogue has long included remixes and alternate versions of previously recorded tracks, while her live shows inevitably find her revisiting and reinventing older songs, which should serve as a healthy reminder that all of these songs are constantly evolving, as Ani fits her lyrics to the expanded possibilities presented by new arrangements, new combinations of instruments, new studio situations. As she has pointed out on several occasions, "the song as you play it on any given day is just that day's interpretation."

And so it is that the fine folks at Hal Leonard, assisted by the eagle eyes of Reg Dickinson (Ani's tireless guitar tech and Keeper of the Tunings) and the aforementioned Ms. Wolf, present you with a cross-section of material— concert favorites as well as songs Ani hasn't played live in a while—reaching all the way back to the 1990 album *Ani DiFranco.* It's an excellent opportunity to take a guided tour behind the scenes as a prolific and adventurous musician learns and refines her craft.

RON EHMKE – RIGHTEOUS BABE RECORDS MINISTER OF COMMUNICATIONS

CONTENTS

Ani DiFranco
1990

BIO

Well over a decade into her career, songwriter, guitarist, and vocalist Ani DiFranco has toured the globe countless times playing to ever-larger and louder audiences, many of whom appear to know every one of her lyrics by heart, including a few she herself has long forgotten. During that time, Ani has released a steady stream of self-produced solo recordings, a pair of collaborations with storyteller Utah Phillips, and numerous side projects on her own label, Righteous Babe Records. In short, she's a perpetually busy grrrl for whom the word "vacation" is simply not an operational concept.

Not So Soft
1991

Imperfectly
1992

"[Ani DiFranco is] a tough and talented singer/songwriter who combines acoustic sensitivity, polyrhythmic energy and millennial consciousness with a do-it-yourself approach to the music business."

—ST. LOUIS [MO] POST DISPATCH

Born in the Rust Belt mecca of Buffalo, New York in 1970, Ani's earliest exposure to music came not from pop radio, but from the folksingers who stayed overnight with her family while making their way across the Northeast. The intimacy and hand-to-mouth economics of the essentially underground folk tradition fueled Ani's own passion for live performance, and she began singing and playing acoustic guitar in Buffalo bars before she turned 10. By age 15, she was writing songs of her own, and soon she was hitting the coffeehouse and club circuit herself. By the time audience members encouraged her to record an album in 1990, Ani had more than 100 original compositions from which to choose: observations about life in her hometown, chronicles of social injustices, journal-like accounts of family dynamics and the politics of the heart. Like countless performers before and after her, Ani chose to release that first cassette herself, without waiting for a label to sign her. Borrowing money from friends, the 20-year-old produced her own self-titled debut album and sold it from the trunk of her car while blazing a trail across the seedy dives and (sometimes seedier) university campuses of North America.

Puddle Dive
1993

Like I Said
1993

Photo by SCOT FISHER

Out of Range
1994

Not a Pretty Girl
1995

Dilate
1996

Little Plastic Castle
1998

Up
Up
Up
Up
Up
Up
1999

Fourth-generation dubs of that tape and its successors sparked interest in Ani from coast to coast, along with ecstatic word of mouth, college and non-commercial radio airplay, and rapturous reviews in zines, college and city papers, and music magazines. Offers from labels large and small poured in, but unlike many young artists under similar circumstances, Ani decided to continue releasing albums herself, which allowed her a far greater degree of artistic freedom than any outside interest would have provided. For Ani, independence is and always has been a political act rather than a marketing option.

Everything happens organically in DiFranco-land. (As Ani puts it, the guiding principle is "Demand before supply.") Both the touring crew and the in-house staff have gradually grown in order to meet increasing need, and Ani's income from concerts, record sales, licensing arrangements, and merchandise is channeled directly back into future projects, which in turn allow her to support like-minded fellow artists, Buffalo businesses, and grassroots activists and culture workers. Perhaps the best example of this process is the appearance of albums recorded by other artists on Righteous Babe, starting with discs by Arto Lindsay, Sekou Sundiata, Sara Lee, and Kurt Swinghammer.

In an era when 5 multinational corporations control 80% of the music industry, Ani is truly on her own and quite happy that way. In her steadfast refusal to compromise her own vision, Ani embodies, as a writer for the *St. Paul Pioneer Press* once put it, "the soul of a shaman, the courage of an activist, and the voice of a generation."

"**If music is meant to influence lives (something that's addressed only when people lobby against the 'wrong' kind of music), then DiFranco fulfilled her activist role at Mud Island. [...] Her stripped-down band—bass, drums, acoustic guitar and keyboards—created a new genre, folk-funk. DiFranco led with a confidant's charisma, investing each song with an emotional payoff that came from passionate vocal phrasing and propulsive guitar work.**"

—THE [MEMPHIS, TN]
COMMERCIAL APPEAL

ANGRY ANYMORE

growing up it was just me and my mom
against the world
and all my sympathies were with her
when i was a little girl
but now i've seen both my parents
play out the hands that they were dealt
and as each year goes by
i know more about how my father must have felt

i just want you to understand
that i know what all the fighting was for
and i just want you to understand
that i'm not angry anymore
i'm not angry anymore

she taught me how to wage a cold war
with quiet charm
but i just want to walk
through my life unarmed
to accept and just get by
like my father learned to do
but without all the acceptance and getting by
that got my father through

night falls like people into love
we generate our own light
to compensate
for the lack of light from above
every time we fight
a cold wind blows our way

but we can learn like the trees
how to bend
how to sway and say

i, i think i understand
what all this fighting is for
and baby, i just want you to understand
that i'm not angry anymore
no, i'm not angry anymore

ANGRY ANYMORE

Words and Music by
ANI DiFRANCO

* Fret number above capo. Capo fret is "0".

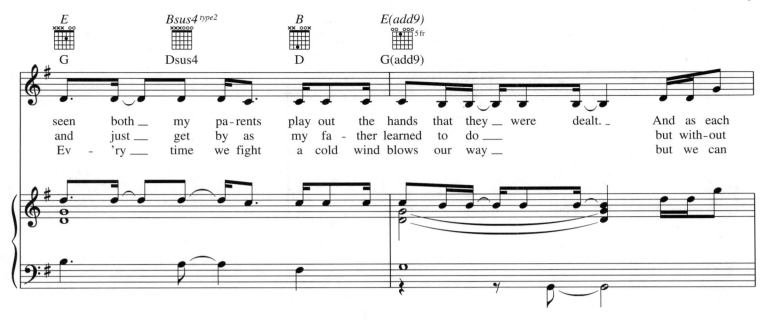

seen both my pa-rents play out the hands that they were dealt. And as each
and just get by as my fa-ther learned to do but with-out
Ev - 'ry time we fight a cold wind blows our way but we can

year goes by I know more a-bout how my fa-ther must have felt.
all the ac-cept-ance and get ting by that got my fa-ther through.
learn like the trees how to bend, how to sway and say

I just want you to un - der - stand that I
I just want you to un - der - stand that I
I, I think I un - der - stand what all this

ANYDAY

i will lean into you
you can be the wind
i will open my mouth
and you can come
rushing in
you can rush in so hard
and make it so i
can't breathe
i breathe too much
anyway
i can do that anyday
i just wish i knew
who you were
i wish you'd
make yourself known
you probably don't realize
i'm her
the woman you want
to call home
i'll keep my ear to the wall
i'll keep my eye on the door
'cause i've heard all
my own jokes
and they're just not funny
anymore
i laugh too much anyway
i can do that anyday
have you ever been bent
or pulled
have you ever been played
like strings
if i could see you
i could strum you
i could break you
make you sing
but i guess you can't really
see the wind
it just comes in and fills the space
and every time something moves
you think that you have
seen its face
and i've always got my guitar
to play
but i can do that anyday

ANYDAY

Words and Music by
ANI DiFRANCO

*Piano plays C(add9) for each instance of this chord.

you can't hide
behind social graces
so don't try
to be all touchy feely
'cuz you lie
in my face of all places
but i got no
problem with that really
what bugs me
is that you believe what you're saying
what bothers me
is that you don't know how you feel
what scares me
is that while you're telling me stories
you actually
believe that they are real
i got no illusions about you
guess what
i never did
when i said
when i said i'll take it
i meant
i meant as is
just give up
and admit you're an asshole
you would be
in some good company
and i think you'd find
that your friends would forgive you
or maybe i
am just speaking for me
when i look around
i think this, this is good enough
and i try to laugh
at whatever life brings
'cuz when i look down
i just miss all the good stuff
and when i look up
i just trip over things
i've got no illusions about you
guess what
i never did
when i say
when i say i'll take it
i mean
i mean as is

aS iS

AS IS

Words and Music by
ANI DiFRANCO

Guitar Tuning; Capo III:

① = D↓ ④ = D
② = B   ⑤ = A
③ = G   ⑥ = E

Moderately

1. You can't hide ___ be - hind ___ so - cial gra -
2.-4. (See additional lyrics)

___ ces.   So don't try ___ to be all touch-y feel - y.

* Fret number above capo. Capoed fret is "0".

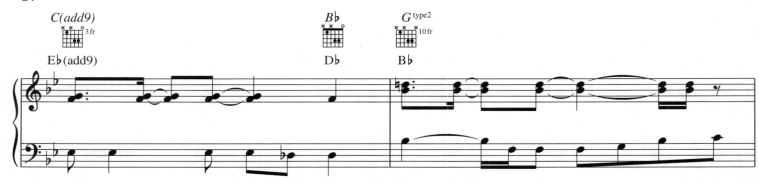

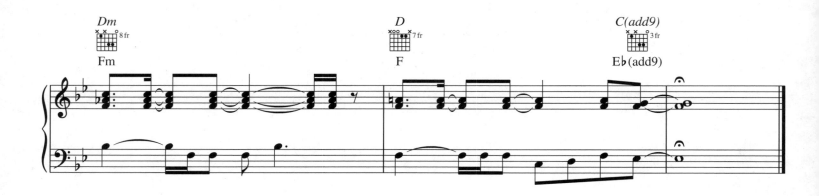

Additional Lyrics

2. What bugs me
   Is that you believe what you're saying.
   What bothers me
   Is that you don't know how you feel.
   What scares me
   Is that while you're telling me stories
   You actually believe that they are real.

   To Chorus:

3. Just give up
   And admit you're an asshole.
   You would be
   In some good company.
   And I think you'd find
   That your friends would forgive you.
   Or maybe I
   Am just speaking for me.

4. Cuz when I look around
   I think this, this is good enough.
   And I try to laugh
   At whatever life brings.
   Cuz when I look down
   I just miss all the good stuff
   And when I look up
   I just trip over things.

   To Chorus:

BOTH HANDS

i am walking out in the rain
i am listening to the low moan of the dial tone
again
i am getting nowhere with you
i can't let it go and i can't get through
the old woman behind the pink curtains
and the closed door
on the first floor
she's listening through the airshaft
to see how long
our swan song can last
both hands
now use both hands
no don't close your eyes
i am writing
graffiti on your body
i am drawing the story
of how hard we tried
i am watching your chest rise and fall
like the tides of my life
and the rest of it all
your bones have been my bed frame
and your flesh has been my pillow
i've been waiting for sleep
to offer up the deep with both hands
in each other's shadow we grew less and less tall
and eventually our theories couldn't explain it all
so i'm recording our history
now on the bedroom wall
and when we leave the landlord will come
and paint over it all

BOTH HANDS

Words and Music by
ANI DiFRANCO

Moderately bright

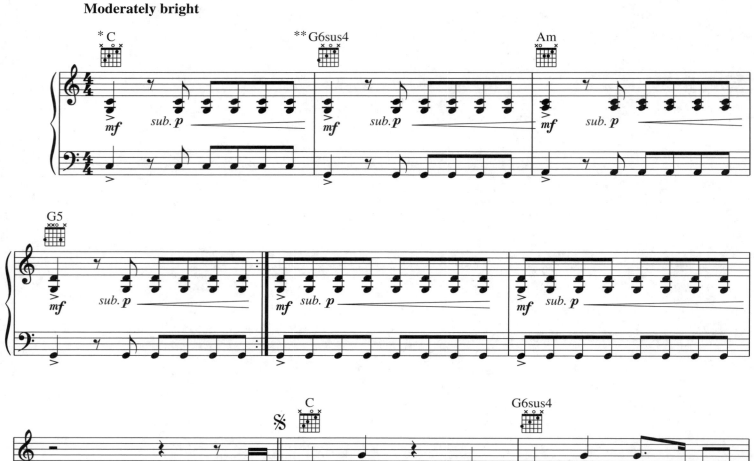

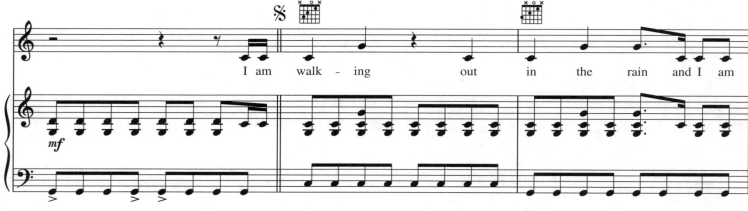

I am walk-ing out in the rain and I am lis-tening to the low __ moan of the di-al tone a-gain. And I am

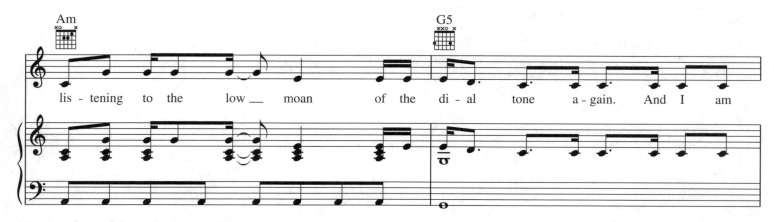

*Piano plays C5 for each instance of this chord.
**Piano plays Gsus4 for each instance of this chord.

*Piano plays Am(add11)

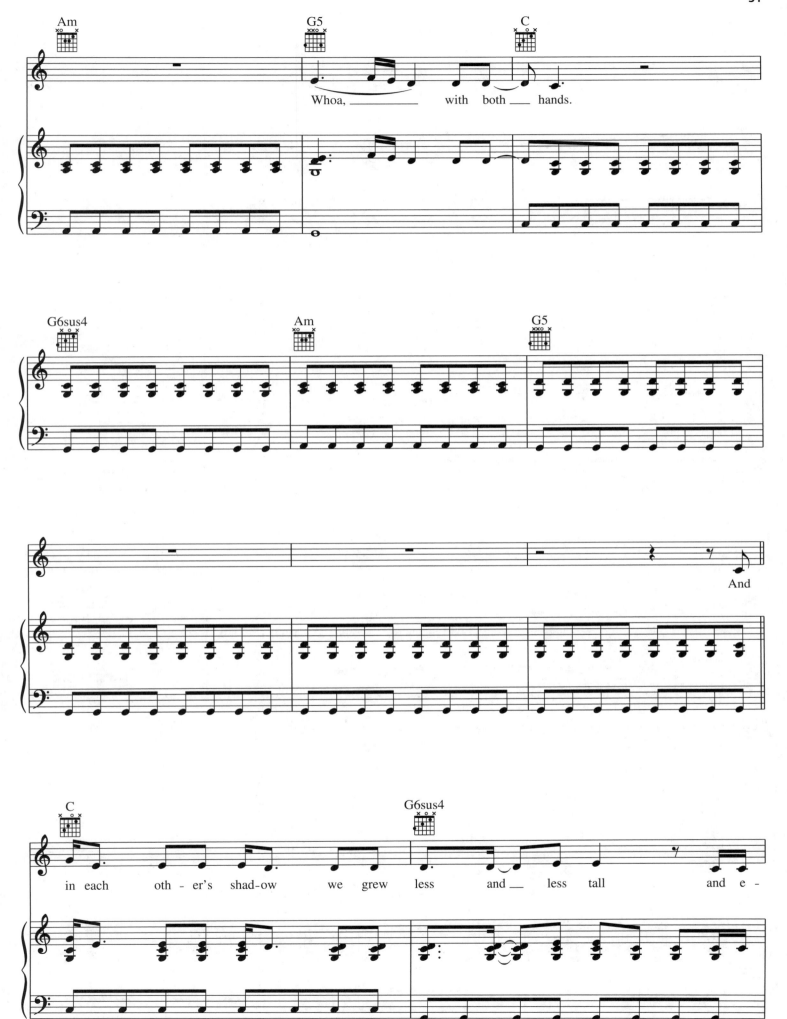

EVEREST

from the depth of the pacific
to the height of everest
and still the world is smoother
than a shiny ball bearing
so i take a few steps back
and put on a wider lens
and it changes your skin
your sex and what you're wearing

distance shows your silhouette
to be a lot like mine
like a sphere is a sphere
and all of us here
have been here all the time
yeah, we've been here all the time

you brought me to church
cinder blocks, fluorescent light
you brought me to church
at seven o'clock on sunday night
and the band was rockin'
and the floors were scrubbed clean
and everybody had a tambourine

so i took a deep breath and became
the white girl with the hair
and you sat right beside me
while everybody stared
and through the open window
i think the singing went outside
and floated up to tell
all the stars not to hide
'cuz by the time church let out
the sky was much clearer
and the moon was so beautiful
that the ocean held up a mirror

as we walked home we spoke slowly
we spoke slow
and we spoke lowly
like it was taking more time
than usual to choose
the words to go
with your squeaky sandal shoes
like time is not a thing
that's ours to lose
from the height of the pacific
to the depth of everest

EVEREST

Words and Music by
ANI DiFRANCO

40

41

FiRE DOOR

i opened the fire door to four lips
none of which were mine
k   i   s   s   i   n   g
tightened my belt around my hips
where your hands are missing
and stepped out in the cold collar high
under the slate grey sky
the air was smoking and the streets were dry
and i wasn't joking when i said goodbye
past magazine quality men talking on the corner
french no less much less of them than us
so why do i feel like something's been rearranged
you know, taken out of context
i must seem so strange
killed a cockroach so big
it left a puddle of pus on my wall
when you and i are lying in bed
you don't seem so tall
and i'm singing now
because my tear ducts are too tired
and my mind is disconnected
but my heart is wired
i make such a good statistic someone should
study me now
someone's got to be interested in how i feel
just because i'm here and i'm real
oh how i miss
substituting the conclusion to a confrontation
with a kiss and
oh how i miss
walking up to the edge and jumping in
like i could feel the future on your skin

FIRE DOOR

Words and Music by
ANI DiFRANCO

Additional Lyrics

2. I killed a cockroach so big
It left a puddle of puss on my wall.
When you and I are lying in bed
You don't seem so tall.
I am singing now
Because my tear ducts are too tired
And my mind is disconnected
But my heart is wired.

To Bridge:

3. Oh, how I miss
Substituting the conclusion to a confrontation
With a kiss and
Oh, how I miss
Walking up to the edge and jumping in
Like I could feel the future on your skin.

thank you
for letting me stay here
thank you
for taking me in
thank you
for the beer and the food
thank you
for loaning me bus fare
thank you
for showing me around
that was a very
kind thing to do
thank you
for the use of the clean towel
thank you
for half of your bed
we can sleep here like
brother and sister you said

but you changed the rules
in an hour or two
i don't know what
you and your sisters do
but please don't
please stop
this is not my obligation
what does my body
have to do
with my gratitude

look at you
little white lying
for the purpose of justifying
what you are trying
to do
i know that you
feel my resistance
i know that you
heard what i said
otherwise you wouldn't need
the excuse

thank you
for letting me stay here
thank you
for taking me in
i don't know where else
i would have gone
but i don't come and go
like a pop song
you can play incessantly
and then forget once it's gone
you can't write me off
and you don't
turn me on

so don't change the rules
in an hour or two
i don't know what you
and your sisters do
but please don't
please stop
this is not my obligation
what does my body
have to do
with my gratitude

GRATITUDE

GRATITUDE

Words and Music by
ANI DiFRANCO

Guitar Tuning:
①= D↓ ④= D
②= B ⑤= A
③= G ⑥= E

Gently

Thank you for let-ting me ___ stay ___ here. ___

Thank you for tak-ing me in. ___ Thank you for the

gRAVeL

i heard the sound of your bike
as your wheels hit the gravel
then your engine in the driveway, cutting off
i pushed through the screen door
and i stood out on the porch
thinking fight fight fight at all costs

but instead i let you in
just like i've always done
i sat you down and offered you a beer
and across the kitchen table
i fired several rounds
but you were still sitting there
when the smoke cleared

you came crawling back to say
that you want to make good in the end
oh, let me count the ways that i abhor you
you were never a good lay
and you were never a good friend
but oh, what can i say, i adore you

all i need is my leather
one t-shirt and two socks
i'll keep my hands warm in your pockets
and you can use the engine block
we'll ride out to california
with my arms around your chest
and i'll pretend that this is real
'cuz this is what i like best

you've been juggling two women
like a stupid circus clown
telling us both we are the one
and maybe you can keep me
from ever being happy
but you're not going to stop me
from having fun

so let's go, before i change my mind
i'll leave the luggage of all your lies behind
'cuz i am bigger than everything that came before
you were never very kind
and you let me way down every time
but oh, what can i say, i adore you

i heard the sound of your bike
as your wheels hit the gravel
then your engine in the driveway, cutting off

GRAVEL

Words and Music by
ANI DiFRANCO

*Piano plays Am/C for each instance of this chord.

To Coda

"Fight, fight, _ fight at all costs." But in -
tend that this _ is real cuz this is what I like best. You've been

stead I let ___ you in just like I've al - ways _ done ___ and I
jug - gling two ___ wom - en like a stu - pid cir - cus clown,

sat you down _ and of - fered you a beer. ___ And a -
tell - ing us ___ both we are the one. ___ And

cross the kitch - en ta - ble I fired sev - 'ral rounds __ but
may - be you ___ can keep me from ev - er be - ing hap - py but

i'M NO HEROINE

you think i wouldn't have him
unless i could have him by the balls
you think i just dish it out
you don't think i take it at all
you think i am stronger
you think i walk taller than the rest
you think i'm usually wearing the pants
just 'cause i rarely wear a dress
well...
when you look at me
you see my purpose you see my pride
you think i just saddle up my anger
and ride and ride and ride
you think i stand so firm
you think i sit so high on my trusty steed
let me tell you
i'm usually face down on the ground
when there's a stampede

i'm no heroine
least not last time i checked
i'm too easy to roll over
i'm too easy to wreck
i just write about what i
should have done
i sing what i wish i could say
and i hope somewhere
some woman hears my music
and it helps her through her day
some guy designed
these shoes i use to walk around
some big man's business
turns a profit everytime
i lay my money down
some guy designed this room
i'm standing in
another one built it
with his own tools
who says i like right angles
these are not my laws
these are not my rules

i'm no heroine
i still answer to the other half
of the race
i don't fool myself like i fooled you
i don't have the power
we just don't run this place

I'M NO HEROINE

Words and Music by
ANI DiFRANCO

Guitar Tuning:
①= E ④= D
②= A↓ ⑤= A
③= G ⑥= E

Brightly

You think I _____ would-n't
When you _____ look at
'Cause some guy _____ de-

D.S. al Coda

I still an-swer to the oth-er half of the race. I don't fool my-self

JUKEBOX

in the jukebox of her memory
the list of names flips by and stops
she closes her eyes
and smiles as the record drops

then she drinks herself up and out
of her kitchen chair
and she dances out of time
as slow as she can sway
for as long as she can say
this dance is mine
this dance is mine

her hair bears silent witness
to the passing of time
tattoos like mile markers
map the distance she has come
winning some, losing some
she says, my sister still calls every sunday night
after the rates go down
but i still can never manage to say anything right
my whole life blew up
and now it's all coming down

she says, leave me alone
tonight i just wanna stay home
she fills the pot with water
and she drops in the bone
she says, i've got a darkness that i have to feed

i've got a sadness
that grows up around me like a weed
and i'm not hurting anyone
i'm just spiraling in
as she closes her eyes
and hears the song begin again

she appreciates the phone calls
the consoling cards and such
she appreciates all the people
who come by and try to pull her back in touch
they try to hold the lid down tightly
and they try to shake well
but the oil and the water
just want to separate themselves

she drinks herself up and out of her kitchen chair
and she dances out of time
as slow as she can sway
for as long as she can say
this dance is mine
this dance is mine
this dance is mine

JUKEBOX

Words and Music by
ANI DiFRANCO

*Gtr. tacet, 1st time, next 8 meas.

She ap - pre - ci - ates ___ the
They try to hold ___ the lid down

phone calls,
tight - ly

the con - sol - ing cards ___ and ___ such.
and they try to shake ___ well.

She ap - pre - ci - ates ___ all the ___ peo - ple ___
But the oil and the ___ wa - ter

who come by ___ and try to pull her back ___ in touch. ___
just want to ___ sep - a - rate them - selves.

LiTTLE pLASTiC CASTLe

in a coffee shop in a city
which is every coffee shop in every city
on a day which is every day
i picked up a magazine
which is every magazine
read a story, and then forgot it right away
they say goldfish have no memory
i guess their lives are much like mine
and the little plastic castle
is a surprise every time
and it's hard to say if they're happy
but they don't seem much to mind
from the shape of your shaved head
i recognized your silhouette
as you walked out of the sun and sat down
and the sight of your sleepy smile
eclipsed all the other people
as they paused to sneer at the two girls
from out of town
i said, look at you this morning
you are, by far, the cutest
but be careful getting coffee
i think these people wanna shoot us
or maybe there's some kinda
local competition here
to see who can be the rudest
people talk
about my image
like i come in two dimensions
like lipstick is a sign of my declining mind
like what i happen to be wearing
the day that someone takes a picture
is my new statement for all of womankind
i wish they could see us now
in leather bras and rubber shorts
like some ridiculous new team uniform
for some ridiculous new sport
quick someone call the girl police
and file a report
in a coffee shop in a city
which is every coffee shop in every city
on a day which is every day

LITTLE PLASTIC CASTLE

Words and Music by
ANI DiFRANCO

*Tenor Guitar Tuning:
① = D ③ = D
② = A ④ = A

Moderately

cof - fee shop   in a cit - y   which is ev - 'ry cof - fee shop
picked up a   mag-a-zine   which is ev - 'ry mag-a-zine.

In a

* To simulate a tenor guitar using a standard 6-string guitar, remove the 1st and 6th strings.
Replace the B and G strings with lighter gauge strings and tune up to D and A, respectively.

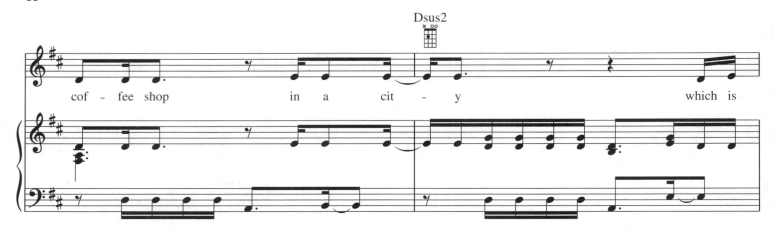

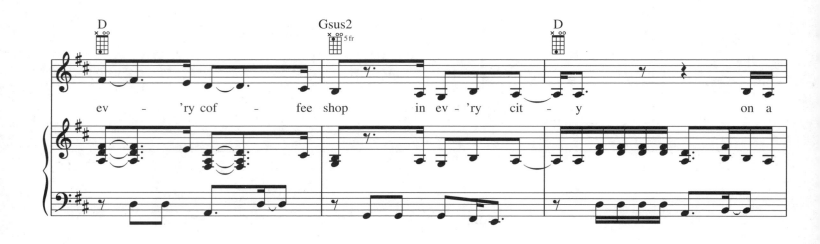

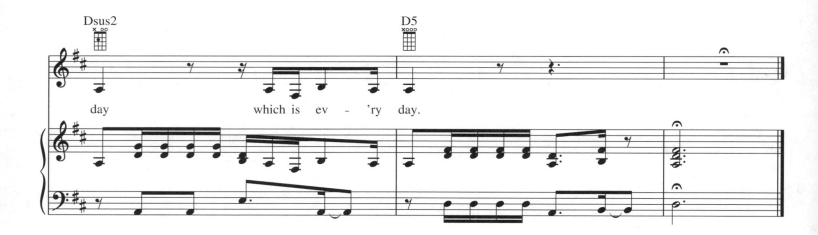

Additional Lyrics

2. And the sight of your sleepy smile eclipsed all the other people
   As they paused to sneer at the two girls from out of town.

   To Chorus:

3. And people talk about my image like I come in two dimensions,
   Like lipstick is a sign of my declining mind.

4. Like what I happen to be wearing the day that someone takes a picture
   Is my new statement for all of womankind, yeah.

   To Chorus:

LOST WOMAN SONG

for lucille clifton

i opened a bank account
when i was nine years old
i closed it when i was eighteen
i gave them every penny that i'd saved
and they gave my blood and my urine a number
now i'm sitting in the waiting room
playing with the toys
i am here to exercise my freedom of choice
i passed their handheld signs
i went through their picket lines
they gathered when they saw me coming
they shouted when they saw me cross
i said why don't you go home
just leave me alone
i'm just another woman lost
you are like fish in the water
who don't know that they are wet
but as far as i can tell
the world isn't perfect yet
his bored eyes were obscene
on his denimed thighs a magazine
i wish he'd never come here with me
in fact i wish he'd never come near me
i wish his shoulder wasn't touching mine
i am growing older waiting in this line
but some of life's best lessons
are learned at the worst times
under the fierce fluorescent
she offered her hand for me to hold
she offered stability and calm
and i was crushing her palm
through the pinch pull wincing
my smile unconvincing
on the sterile battlefield that sees
only casualties
never heroes

my heart hit absolute zero
lucille, your voice still sounds in me
mine was a relatively easy tragedy
the profile of our country
looks a little less hard-nosed
but that picket line persisted
and that clinic has since been closed
they keep pounding their fists on reality
hoping it will break
but i don't think that there's one of them
who leads a life free of mistakes

LOST WOMAN SONG

Words and Music by
ANI DiFRANCO

Guitar Tuning:
① = D♭ ④ = D
② = B   ⑤ = A
③ = G   ⑥ = E

Moderately bright

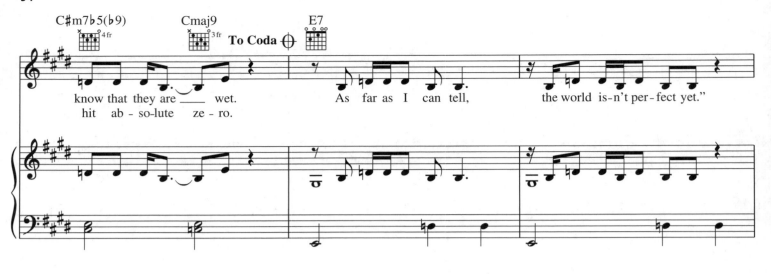

know that they are ___ wet.
hit ab - so - lute ze - ro.
As far as I can tell,
the world is-n't per-fect yet."

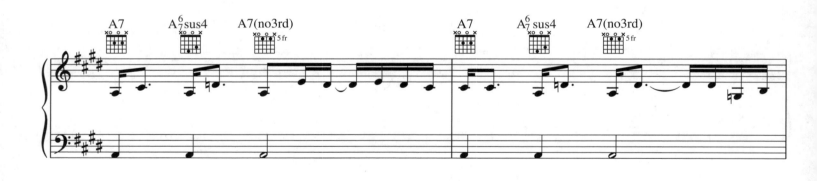

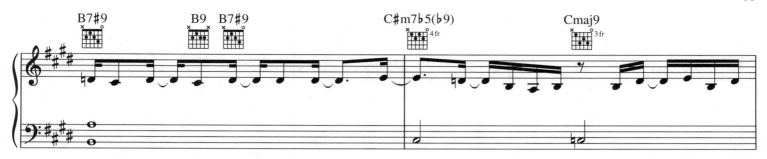

D.S. al Coda

And his

CODA

And Lu -

cille, your voice still sounds in me. _ Yeah, mine was a rel - a-tive - ly

they told you your music
could reach millions
that the choice was up to you
and you told me they always
pay for lunch
and they believe in what i do
and i wonder
will you miss your old friends
once you've proven what you're worth
yeah i wonder
when you're a big star
will you miss the earth

i knew you would always want more
i knew you would never be done
'cuz everyone is a fucking napoleon
yeah everyone is a fucking napoleon

and the next time
that i saw you
you were larger than life
you came and you conquered
you were doing alright
you had an army
of suits behind you
all you had to be was willing
and i said i still
make a pretty good living
but you must make a killing
a killing

i hope that you are happy
i hope at least you are having fun
'cuz everyone is a fucking napoleon
yeah everyone is a fucking napoleon

now you think, so that is
the way it's gonna be
that's what this is all about
and i think that is
the way it always was
you chose not to notice until now
yeah now that there's a problem
you call me up to confide
and you go on for over an hour
'bout each one that took you for a ride

and i guess that you dialed my number
'cuz you thought for sure that i'd agree
and i say baby, you know i still love you
but how dare you complain to me

everyone is a fucking napoleon
yeah everyone is a fucking napoleon

NAPOLEON

NAPOLEON

Words and Music by
ANI DiFRANCO

OVERLAP

i search your profile for a translation
                    i study the conversation like a map
'cause i know there is strength
                    in the differences between us
and i know there is comfort
                    where we overlap

            come here
                    stand in front of the light
            stand still
                    so i can see your silhouette
                i hope
                    that you have got all night
'cause i'm not done looking yet

                    each one of us
        wants a piece of the action
                    you can hear it in what we say
    you can see it in what we do
                    we negotiate with chaos
    for some sense of satisfaction
                    if you won't give it to me
    at least give me a better view

                    come here
            stand in front of the light
                    stand still
        so i can see your silhouette
                    i hope
        that you have got all night
                    'cause i'm not done looking yet

i build each one of my songs out of glass
                    so you could see me inside them i suppose
    or you could just leave the image of me
                    in the background i guess
and watch your own reflection superimposed

                    i build each one of my days out of hope
        and i give that hope your name
                    and i don't know you that well
    but it don't take much to tell
                    either you don't have the balls
        or you don't feel the same

                    come here
            stand in front of the light
                    stand still
        so i can see your silhouette
                    i hope
        that you have got all night
                    'cause i'm not done looking yet

i search your profile for a translation
                    and i study the conversation like a map
        'cause i know there is strength
                    in the differences between us
        and i know there is comfort
                    where we overlap

OVERLAP

Words and Music by
ANI DiFRANCO

* Play Bm(add9)^type2, 2nd time.

** Play Bm(add 2/4), 2nd time; Bm(add9)^type2, 3rd time.

* Play Bm(add9), 2nd & 3rd times.

* Play Bm(add $\frac{2}{4}$), 3rd time.

To Coda

SHE SAYS

she says forget what you have to do
pretend there is nothing
outside this room
and like an idea she came to me
but she came too late
or maybe too soon
i said please try not to love me
close your eyes
i'm turning on the light
you know i have no vacancy
and it's awfully cold outside tonight
the rain stains the brick
a darker red
slowly i'm rolling
out of the bed
the rain stains the street
a darker black
i dress my face in stone
because i can't go back
i feel her eyes watching me
from behind the curtain of her hair
she says i'm sorry
i didn't mean to stare
i say i think i really have to go now
but oh baby maybe someday
maybe somehow

SHE SAYS

Words and Music by
ANI DiFRANCO

3² FLAVORs

squint your eyes and look closer
i'm not between you and your ambition
i am a poster girl with no poster
i am thirty-two flavors and then some
and i'm beyond your peripheral vision
so you might wanna turn your head
'cuz some day you are going to get hungry
and eat most of the words you just said

both my parents taught me about good will
and i have done well by their names
just the kindness i've lavished on strangers
is more than i can explain
still there's many
who've turned out their porch lights
just so i would think they were not home
and hid in the dark of their windows
'til i passed and left them alone

god help you if you are an ugly girl
course too pretty is also your doom
'cuz everyone harbors a secret hatred
for the prettiest girl in the room
and god help you if you are a phoenix
and you dare to rise up from the ash
a thousand eyes will smolder with jealousy
while you are just flying past

i never tried to give my life meaning
by demeaning you
and i would like to state for the record
i did everything that i could do
i'm not saying that i'm a saint
i just don't wanna live that way
i will never be a saint
but i will always say

squint your eyes and look closer
i'm not between you and your ambition
i am a poster girl with no poster
i am thirty-two flavors and then some
and i'm beyond your peripheral vision
so you might wanna turn your head
'cuz some day you might find you are starving
and eating all of the words that you said

32 FLAVORS

Words and Music by
ANI DiFRANCO

they caught the last poor man
on a poor man's vacation
they cuffed him and they confiscated his stuff
they dragged his black ass down to the station
and said, o.k., the streets are safe now
all your pretty white children can come out and see spot run
and they came out of their houses
and they looked around
but they didn't see no one

my country 'tis of thee
to take swings at each other on the talk-show tv
why don't you just go ahead and turn off the sun
'cuz we'll never live long enough
to undo everything they've done to you
undo everything they've done to you

above 96th street
they're handin' out smallpox blankets so people don't freeze
the old dogs have got a new trick
it's called criminalize the symptoms
while you spread the disease
and i hold on hard to something
between my teeth when i'm sleeping
i wake up and my jaw aches
and the earth is full of earthquakes

my country 'tis of thee
to take shots at each other on the primetime tv
why don't you just go ahead and turn off the sun
'cuz we'll never live long enough
to undo everything they've done to you
undo everything they've done to you

they caught the last poor man
flying away in a shiny red cape
they took him down to the station
and they said, boy you should've known better
than to try to escape
i ran away with the circus
'cuz there's still some honest work left for bearded ladies
but it's not the same going town to town
since they put everyone in jail
except the cleavers and the bradys
my country 'tis of thee
to take swings at each other on the talk-show tv
why don't you just go ahead and turn off the sun
'cuz we'll never live long enough
to undo everything they've done to you
undo everything they've done to you

'TIS OF THEE

Words and Music by
ANI DiFRANCO

* Fret number above capo. Capoed fret is "0".

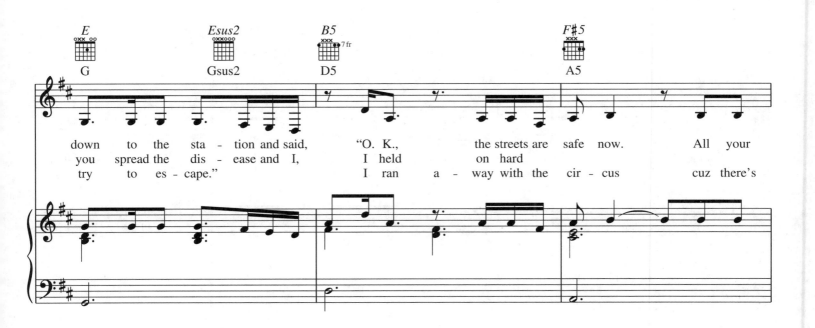

pret - ty white chil - dren can come out and see Spot run." And they came out of their
to some thing be - tween my teeth when I'm sleep - ing. I wake up and my
still some hon - est work left for beard - ed la - dies. But it's not the same, go - ing town

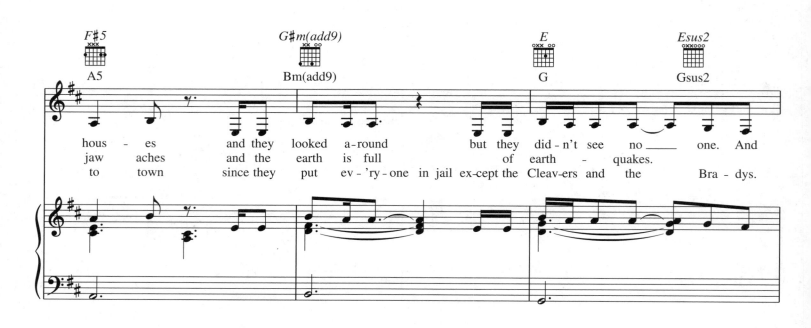

hous - es and they looked a - round but they did - n't see no _____ one. And
jaw aches and the earth is full of earth - quakes.
to town since they put ev - 'ry - one in jail ex - cept the Cleav - ers and the Bra - dys.

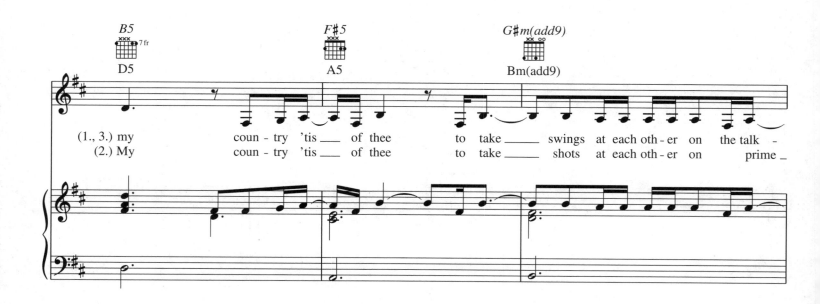

(1., 3.) my coun - try 'tis _____ of thee to take _____ swings at each oth - er on the talk -
(2.) My coun - try 'tis _____ of thee to take _____ shots at each oth - er on prime _

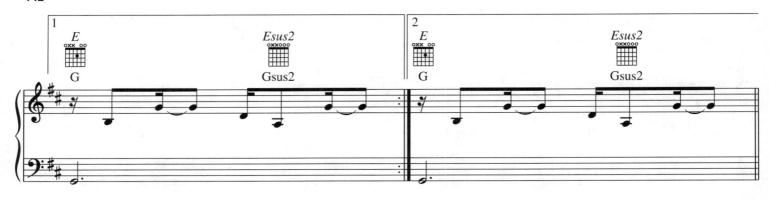

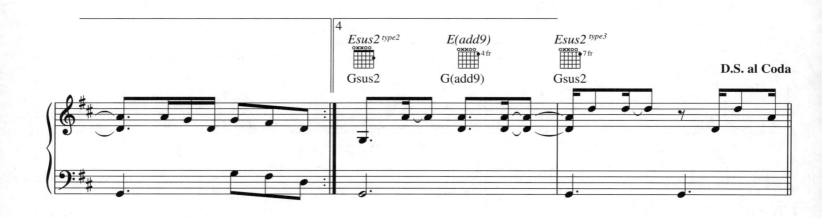

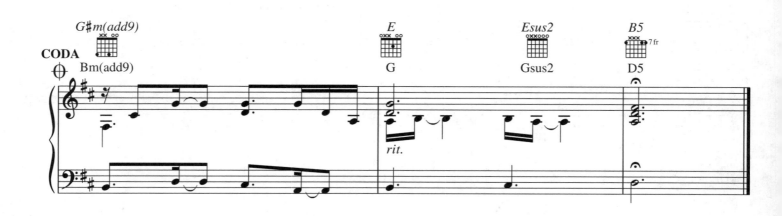

TWO LITTLE GIRLS

and you know i would prefer
if she didn't empty her syringes
into your arm

here comes little naked me
padding up to the bathroom door
to find little naked you
slumped on the bathroom floor
so i guess i'll just stand here
with my back against the wall
while you distill your whole life
down to a 911 call

now you bring me your bruises
so i can 'ooh and ahh' at the display
maybe i'm supposed to make one of my famous jokes
that makes everything o.k.
or maybe i'm supposed to be the handsome prince
who rides up and unties your hands
or maybe i'm supposed to be the furrowed-brow friend
who thinks she understands

you were fresh off the boat
from virginia
i had a year of new york city
under my belt
we met in a dream
we were both nineteen
i remember where we were standing
i remember how it felt
two little girls
growing out of their training bras
this little girl breaks furniture
this little girl breaks laws
two girls together
just a little less alone
this little girl cried wee wee wee
all the way home

here comes little naked me
padding up to the bathroom door
to find little naked you
slumped on the bathroom floor
so i guess i'll just stand here
with my back against the wall
while you distill your whole life
down to a 911 call

you were always half crazy
now look at you baby
you make about as much sense
as a nursery rhyme
love is a piano
dropped from a four story window
and you were in the wrong place
at the wrong time
and i don't like your girlfriend
i blame her
i never seen one of your lovers
do you so much harm
i loved you first

TWO LITTLE GIRLS

Words and Music by
ANI DiFRANCO

*Piano plays Em7♭5

*Piano plays B♭maj7
**Piano plays C(add11)/G for each instance of this chord.

This lit-tle girl cried, "Wee, wee,__ wee," all the __ way

if she did-n't emp-ty her sy - rin - ges in-to your arms. __

home. ____

Ah. ____

Ah. ____

So now you bring me ____ your bruis- es so I can ooh and aah at the dis- play.

UNTOUCHABLE fACE

think i'm going for a walk now
i feel a little unsteady
don't want nobody to follow me
'cept maybe you
i could make you happy, y'know
if you weren't already
i could do a lot of things
and i do

tell you the truth i prefer
the worst of you
too bad you had to have a better half
she's not really my type
but i think you two are forever
and i hate to say it
but you're perfect together

so fuck you
and your untouchable face
and fuck you
for existing in the first place
who am i
that i should be vying for your touch
who am i
bet you can't even tell me that much

two-thirty in the morning
and my gas tank will be empty soon
neon sign on the horizon
rubbing elbows with the moon
a safe haven of sleepless
where the deep fryer's always on
and the radio is counting down
the top twenty country songs
and out on the porch the fly strip
is waving like a flag in the wind

y'know, i don't look forward
to seeing you again
you'll look like a photograph of yourself
taken from far far away
and i won't know what to do
and i won't know what to say

except fuck you
and your untouchable face
and fuck you
for existing in the first place
who am i
that i should be vying for your touch
who am i
bet you can't even tell me that much

i see you and i'm so perplexed
what was i thinking
what will i think of next
where can i hide
in the back room there's a lamp
that hangs over the pool table
and when the fan is on it swings
gently side to side
there's a changing constellation
of balls as we are playing
i see orion and say nothing
the only thing i can think of saying

is fuck you
and your untouchable face
and fuck you
for existing in the first place
who am i
that i should be vying for your touch
who am i
bet you can't even tell me that much

UNTOUCHABLE FACE

Words and Music by
ANI DiFRANCO

*Piano plays Em for this chord

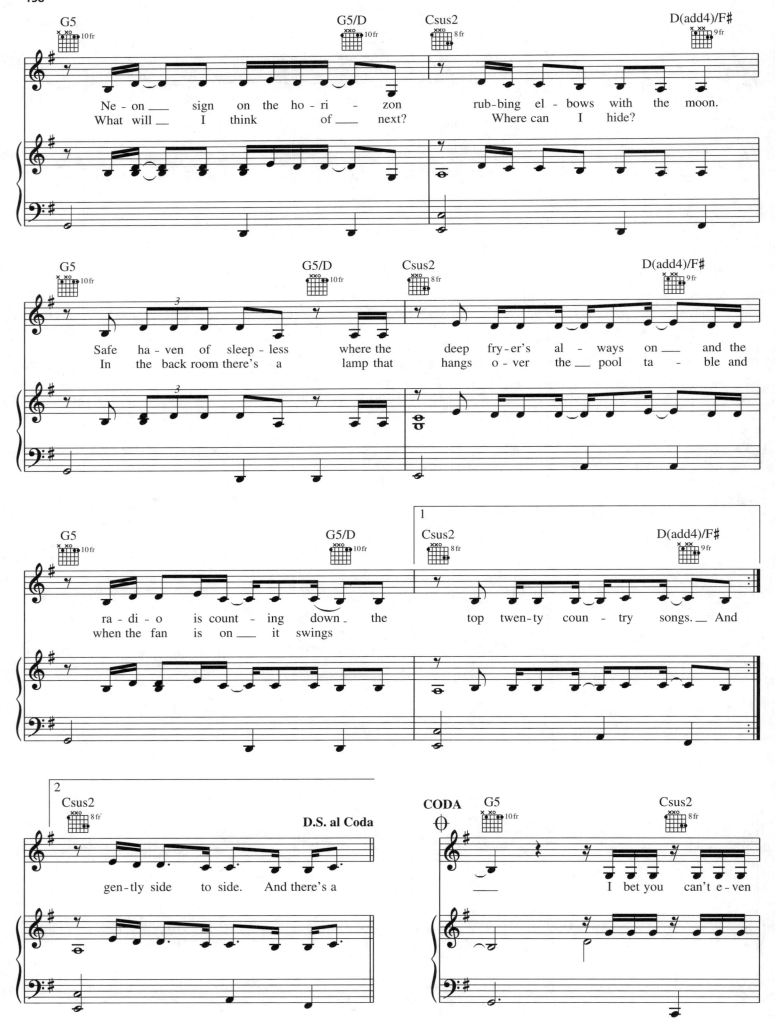

WILLING to FIGHT

the windows of my soul
are made of one way glass
don't bother looking into my eyes
if there's something
you want to know just ask
i got a dead bolt stroll
where i'm going is clear
i won't wait for you
to wonder
i'll just tell you why
i'm here
'cause i know the
biggest crime
is to just throw
up your hands
say this has nothing
to do with me
i just want to live
as comfortably
as i can
you got to look outside
your eyes
you got to think outside
your brain
you got to walk outside
your life
to where the neighborhood
changes tell me

who's your boogie man
that's who i will be
you don't have to like me
for who i am but we'll see
what you're made of by
what you make of me
i think it's absurd that you think i
am the derelict daughter
i fight fire with words
words are hotter than flames
words are wetter than water
i got friends all over this country
i got friends in other countries too
i got friends i haven't met yet
i got friends i never knew
i got lovers whose eyes
i've only seen at a glance
i got strangers
for great grandchildren
i got strangers for ancestors
i was a long time coming i'll be a
long time gone
you got your whole life to do something
and that's not very long
so why don't you give me a call
when you decide you're willing to fight
for what you think is real
for what you think is right

WILLING TO FIGHT

Words and Music by
ANI DiFRANCO

* Fret number above capo. Capoed fret is "0."

what you think is right. ___

how can i go home
with nothing to say
i know you're going to look at me that way
and say what did you do out there
and what did you decide
you said you needed time
and you had time

you are a china shop and i am a bull
you are really good food and i am full
i guess everything's timing
i guess everything's been said
so i am coming home with an empty head

you'll say did they love you or what
and i'll say they love what i do
the only one who really loves me is you
and you'll say girl did you kick some butt
and i'll say i don't really remember
but my fingers are sore
and my voice is too

you'll say it's really good to see you
you'll say i missed you horribly
you'll say let me carry that
give that to me
and you will take the heavy stuff
and you will drive the car
and i'll look out the window and make jokes
about the way things are

how can i go home
with nothing to say
i know you're going to look at me that way
and say what did you do out there
what did you decide
you said you needed time
and you had time

YOU HAD TIME

YOU HAD TIME

Words and Music by
ANI DiFRANCO

Original key: F♯ major. This edition has been transposed up one half-step to be more playable.
* Capo IV to match recording (2:06).

* Fret number above capo. Capoed fret is "0."